Reach
HIGHER

Practice Book

NATIONAL GEOGRAPHIC LEARNING

Australia · Brazil · Mexico · Singapore · United Kingdom · United States

National Geographic Learning,
a Cengage Company

Reach Higher Practice Book 3A

Publisher, Content-based English: Erik Gundersen

Associate Director, R&D: Barnaby Pelter

Senior Development Editors:
  Jacqueline Eu
  Ranjini Fonseka
  Kelsey Zhang

Development Editor: Rayne Ngoi

Director of Global Marketing: Ian Martin

Heads of Regional Marketing:
  Charlotte Ellis (Europe, Middle East and Africa)
  Kiel Hamm (Asia)
  Irina Pereyra (Latin America)

Product Marketing Manager: David Spain

Senior Production Controller: Tan Jin Hock

Senior Media Researcher (Covers): Leila Hishmeh

Senior Designer: Lisa Trager

Director, Operations: Jason Seigel

Operations Support:
  Rebecca Barbush
  Drew Robertson
  Caroline Stephenson
  Nicholas Yeaton

Manufacturing Planner: Mary Beth Hennebury

Publishing Consultancy and Composition:
  MPS North America LLC

© 2020 Cengage Learning, Inc.

ALL RIGHTS RESERVED. No part of this work covered by the copyright herein may be reproduced or distributed in any form or by any means, except as permitted by U.S. copyright law, without the prior written permission of the copyright owner.

"National Geographic", "National Geographic Society" and the Yellow Border Design are registered trademarks of the National Geographic Society ® Marcas Registradas

For permission to use material from this text or product, submit all requests online at **cengage.com/permissions**
Further permissions questions can be emailed to
permissionrequest@cengage.com

ISBN-13: 978-0-357-36688-2

National Geographic Learning
200 Pier Four Blvd
Boston, MA 02210
USA

Locate your local office at **international.cengage.com/region**

Visit National Geographic Learning online at **ELTNGL.com**
Visit our corporate website at **www.cengage.com**

Printed in the United States of America
Print Number: 12   Print Year: 2024

Contents

Unit 3: Life in the Soil

Unit 4: Let's Work Together

Name _____   Date _____

Happy to Help

Make a concept map with the answers to the Big Question:
How do people help each other?

How people
help
each other

Thinking Map

Someone Who Needs Help
Make a story map about someone you know who needs help.

Beginning:

↓

Middle:

↓

End:

Use the story map to retell your story to a partner.

Grammar

A Day at the Park

Grammar Rules Complete Sentences

A **complete sentence** expresses a complete thought. It has a subject and a predicate.

The **subject** tells who or what does something.

The **predicate** tells what the subject does.

The subject usually comes first in a sentence. The predicate usually comes second.

Example: *The people* *built a nice park.*

               ↑   ↑

     subject   **predicate**

Read each sentence part. Draw a line to match each subject with a predicate.

Subject	Predicate
1. Tanya	**a.** gather acorns.
2. The birds	**b.** come to play with Tanya.
3. Two squirrels	**c.** plays in the park.
4. Some friends	**d.** shines brightly in the sky.
5. The sun	**e.** fly from tree to tree.

 Tell a partner how you decided which predicate to match with each subject.

Name _____   Date _____

"Those Shoes"

Listen as your teacher reads. Follow with your finger.

All of Jeremy's friends at school have black shoes. Jeremy wants a pair very much.

Jeremy needs a pair of boots for winter. Grandma says they should only buy things that they need.

One day, Jeremy's shoes tear. Jeremy gets shoes with cartoon animals. The kids laugh at his cartoon shoes.

Jeremy and Grandma go to stores that sell old clothes. They look for the black shoes. He finds some, but they are too small. Jeremy buys them anyway. He hopes the shoes will stretch, but they do not. He has to wear the cartoon shoes instead.

Jeremy knows that Antonio needs new shoes. He gives Antonio his black shoes. Jeremy wears the shoes with the cartoon animals. Antonio thanks Jeremy. Jeremy and Antonio become friends.

Get Well Soon!

Grammar Rules Capital Letters

A complete sentence always begins with a **capital letter**.

Example:

Don't write:
my friend needed help.

Write:
My *friend needed help.*

Circle the letters that should be capitals. Then write the sentences correctly in a paragraph.

> my friend Anna has a cold.
>
> i bring some soup to her house.
>
> she eats the soup.
>
> now she feels better!
>
> her mother thanks me.

_____

_____

_____

_____

Tell a partner why you added each capital letter.

Vocabulary

Vocabulary Bingo

Play Bingo using the Key Words from this unit.

Name _____ Date _____

"Those Shoes"

Make a story map for "Those Shoes."

Beginning:

First, Jeremy wants new shoes, but they cost too much.

↓

Middle:

Next, Jeremy buys shoes that are too small.

↓

Then, _____.

_____

_____

↓

End:

Finally, _____.

_____

_____

Use your story map to summarize the story's plot to a partner.

Compound Words

gold fish   sail boat

Connect two smaller words to make the compound word that names the picture. Write the compound word on the line.

1. dish butter fly _____	2. shine sun flower _____
3. board skate park _____	4. plane air port _____
5. flake snow bank _____	6. drop rain coat _____

Read the sentence. Underline the compound words. Draw a line between the two smaller words in each compound word.

The snowflake fell on the snowbank and melted in the sunshine.

Fluency

"Those Shoes"

Use this passage to practice reading with proper expression.

I have dreams about those shoes. Black high-tops.	8
Two white stripes.	11
"Grandma, I want them."	15
"There's no room for 'want' around here," Grandma says.	24
"What you *need* are new boots for winter."	32

From "Those Shoes," page 14

Expression

B ☐ Does not read with feeling.   A ☐ Reads with appropriate feeling with most content.

I ☐ Reads with some feeling, but does not match content.   AH ☐ Reads with appropriate feeling for all content.

Accuracy and Rate Formula

Use the formula to measure a reader's accuracy and rate while reading aloud.

$$\underline{\hspace{3cm}} - \underline{\hspace{3cm}} = \underline{\hspace{3cm}}$$

words attempted in one minute	number of errors	words correct per minute (wcpm)

Name _____   Date _____

"Guardian Angel"

Complete the dialogue journal as you read "Guardian Angel."

What I think	What my partner thinks
Page _____	_____
_____	_____
_____	_____
_____	_____
Page _____	_____
_____	_____
_____	_____
_____	_____
Page _____	_____
_____	_____
_____	_____
_____	_____

Tell a partner what you would do to help a new student in class feel more welcome.

Name _____   Date _____

Compare Genres

Use the checklist chart to compare a story and a poem.

	Story	Poem
It is arranged in lines.		✓
It has paragraphs.	✓	
It is usually long.		
It is usually short.		
It expresses the writer's feelings.		
The words sound like music.		

Take turns with a partner. Ask each other questions about a story or poem.

© Cengage Learning, Inc.

Grammar

Where's the Kitten?

Grammar Rules Complete Sentences

A **complete sentence** expresses a complete thought. It has a
subject and a **predicate**.

Example: _A young girl_ _has a small kitten._
                        ↑   ↑
                  subject   **predicate**

**Circle the complete sentence in each pair. Then copy the correct
sentences on the lines below to make a story.**

1.	My friend Maria.	My friend Maria has a kitten.
2.	The kitten ran away.	Ran away.
3.	Looked everywhere.	Maria looked everywhere.
4.	Her sister Lisa helped her.	Her sister Lisa.
5.	The girls found the kitten!	Found the kitten!

_____

_____

_____

_____

Tell a partner about how you know each sentence is complete.

Something That Has Improved

Make a comparison chart about something that has improved.

Before	Now

Tell a partner how you improved something. Tell how the thing was before and how it is now. Use the words **before, then, now, and after** to compare.

Grammar

Soup's On, Kemal!

Grammar Rules Complete Subjects and Predicates

The **complete subject** is all of the words that tell who or what does something.

The **complete predicate** is all of the words that tell what the subject does.

Remember, a sentence always begins with a capital letter.

Example: *A volunteer* *helps at a soup kitchen.*

complete subject   **complete predicate**

Read each group of words. Combine complete subjects and complete predicates to make sentences. Write the sentences on the lines.

a soup kitchen	tastes good
many individuals	feeds many people
a dish of rice	serve the food

1. _____

2. _____

3. _____

 Talk with a partner about why each complete subject and complete predicate belong together.

© Cengage Learning, Inc.

Name _____ Date _____

"The World's Greatest Underachiever"

Listen as your teacher reads. Follow with your finger.

1

Henry Winkler wanted to get good grades in school. He studied a lot, but he forgot things easily. He did not give up. He tried to improve his grades.

2

Henry felt bad about himself. He tried very hard, but people told him he was stupid or lazy.

3

Henry grew up and became an actor. He also had a son named Jed. Teachers discovered that Jed had dyslexia. This means that his brain learns things in a different way. Then Henry understood that he had dyslexia, too.

4

Today, Henry talks to other kids about his life. He says to find out what makes you special and share it with the world.

© Cengage Learning, Inc.

Grammar

A Helping Paw

Grammar Rules **Simple Subjects and Predicates**

The **simple subject** is the most important word in the subject. The **simple predicate** is the most important word in the predicate. The simple predicate is often an action word.

When the simple subject is one person or thing and the simple predicate shows action that happens now, the simple predicate ends in **-s**.
Example: *The perky dog trots to the door.*

When the simple subject is more than one person or thing, the simple predicate that happens now does not end in **-s**.
Example: *The happy dogs arrive at the neighborhood hospital.*

Read each sentence. Circle the correct form of the simple predicate.

1. A pet owner (take | takes) her dog to visit sick people.
2. The nurses (like | likes) many dogs to visit patients.
3. The friendly dog (place | places) her head next to a patient.
4. A hospital aide (smile | smiles) at the friendly dog.
5. Many relatives (request | requests) visits for their sick family member.

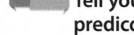 **Tell your partner how you decided which form of the simple predicate to circle.**

Name _____ Date _____

Comparing Henry

Use a comparison chart to show how Henry changed in "The World's Greatest Underachiever."

Before	Now
1. Henry had trouble spelling.	**1.** Henry writes *books*.
2. He didn't like school.	**2.**
3.	**3.**
4.	**4.**
5.	**5.**

Use your comparison chart to retell the selection to a partner.
Use: *Before, Henry* _____. *Now, he* _____.

1.17

Phonics Practice

Syllable Division

cat   rab/bit   pup/py

Read each word. Draw a line between the syllables in the two-syllable words. Circle the word that names the picture.

1.		muffin most	**2.**	50	fifteen fifty
3.		hammer hamper	**4.**		apple apply
5.		guard garden	**6.**		pan practice

Read the sentences. Underline the two-syllable words and write them in the chart. Circle the two-syllable words that are compound words.

1. The cupcake was yummy.

2. My puppy's name is Sunshine.

3. I put the letter in the mailbox.

4. We had muffins at the picnic.

Two-syllable words	

Name _____ Date _____

"The World's Greatest Underachiever"

Use this passage to practice reading with proper intonation.

The next day, I went into the classroom and took out a sheet of paper.	15
Then Miss Adolf gave us the words. The first word was *carpet*.	27
I wrote that one down: *c-a-r-p-e-t*. I was feeling pretty confident.	38
Then came *neighbor*—I wrote down the letter *n*.	47
Then *rhythm*—I knew there was an *r. Suburban*—I wrote *s-u-b*.	59
My heart sank.	62
I had gone from 100 percent to maybe a D-minus.	72
Where did the words go?	77

From "The World's Greatest Underachiever," pages 50–51

Intonation

- **B** ☐ Does not change pitch.
- **I** ☐ Changes pitch, but does not match content.
- **A** ☐ Changes pitch to match some of the content.
- **AH** ☐ Changes pitch to match all of the content.

Accuracy and Rate Formula

Use the formula to measure a reader's accuracy and rate while reading aloud.

_____ − _____ = _____
words attempted   number of errors   words correct per minute
in one minute   (wcpm)

Reading Options

"Joseph Lekuton: Making a Difference"

Complete the reflection journal as you read "Joseph Lekuton: Making a Difference."

Page	Question	Answer

 Work with a small group. Compare your questions and answers with those of other students. Explain how you figured out two of your answers.

Name _____ Date _____

Compare Points of View

Use the comparison chart to compare a biography and an autobiography.

"The World's Greatest Underachiever"	"Joseph Lekuton: Making a Difference"
The narrator tells the story of _____ life.	The narrator tells the story of _____ life.
The narrator is/is not part of the story. (Circle one.)	The narrator is/is not part of the story. (Circle one.)
The selection is an autobiography/ a biography. (Circle one.)	The selection is an autobiography/ a biography. (Circle one.)
Examples of narrator's point of view:	Examples of narrator's point of view:

▶ Take turns with a partner. Describe ways you know that a selection is a biography or an autobiography.

Name _____ Date _____

Grammar

We Like to Read

Grammar Rules Adding -s to Action Verbs

Use **-s** at the end of an action verb if the subject is **he**, **she**, or **it**.	*Danny reads a story.* *He looks at the pictures.*
Do not use **-s** for **I**, **you**, **we**, or **they**.	*I read to my friends.* *They look at the pictures.*

Read each sentence. Write the correct form of the verb for each subject.

1. We _____ many stories.

read/reads

2. I _____ autobiographies.

like/likes

3. They _____ about real people.

tell/tells

4. Henry Winkler _____ his own story.

tell/tells

5. He _____ his problems in school.

remember/remembers

6. His brain _____ differently.

learn/learns

7. You _____ autobiographies, too.

like/likes

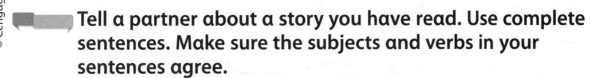 **Tell a partner about a story you have read. Use complete sentences. Make sure the subjects and verbs in your sentences agree.**

© Cengage Learning, Inc.

1.22

Unit 1 | Happy to Help

Grammar

The *Be* Verb Game

Grammar Rules Subject-Verb Agreement: *Be*

When you tell what someone or something is now:

- Use **am** after the subject **I**.   *I **am** helpful.*
- Use **is** after the subjects **he**,   *He **is** a volunteer.*
  she, and **it**.
- Use **are** after the subjects   *You **are** a good neighbor.*
  you, **we**, and **they**.   *They **are** good friends.*

1. Play with a partner.
2. Spin the spinner.
3. Use the word as a subject. Say a sentence with a **be** verb.

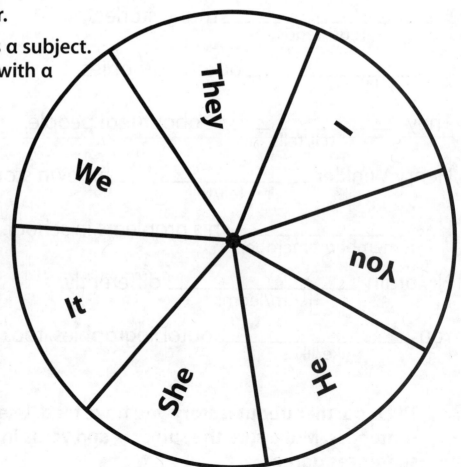

Make a Spinner

1. Place one loop of a paper clip over the center of the circle.
2. Push a sharp pencil through the loop and the paper.
3. Spin the paper clip around the pencil.

Writing Project

Voice

Every writer has a special way of saying things, or a voice. The voice should sound genuine, or real, and be unique to that writer.

	Does the writing sound genuine and unique?	**Does the tone fit the audience and purpose?**
4 Wow!	❑ The writing is genuine and unique. It shows who the writer is.	❑ The writer's tone, formal or informal, fits the audience and purpose.
3 Ahh.	❑ Most of the writing sounds genuine and unique.	❑ The writer's tone mostly fits the audience and purpose.
2 Hmm.	❑ Some of the writing sounds genuine and unique.	❑ Some of the writing fits the audience and purpose.
1 Huh?	❑ The writing does not sound genuine or unique.	❑ The writer's tone does not fit the audience or purpose.

Name _____ Date _____

Story Map

Complete the story map for your personal narrative.

Beginning:

Middle:

End:

Writing Project

Revise

Use revision marks to make changes to this paragraph. Look for:

- **a personal voice**
- **vivid words**

Revision Marks	
∧	Add
ℛ	Take out
⬭⤴	Move to here

It was the first day of school. The new girl looked scared.

Another girl went to her and helped her. She showed her to the

right classroom. They ate lunch together. They became friends.

Writing Project

Edit and Proofread

Use revision marks to edit and proofread this paragraph. Look for:

- complete sentences
- capitalization and punctuation
- correct spelling

	Revision Marks
∧	Add
ꝗ	Take out
⟳↷	Move to here
⬭	Check spelling
≡	Capitalize
∧	Insert period

I was late to school mom droped me off at the front steps.

I grabbed my bag and ran My bag was open, though, and my

papers spilled all over the ground! I watched them fly in different

directions, and I wanted to cry. Just then Isabella appeared.

scooped up my papers and walked over to me. I was so hapy. She

saved my day!

Unit Concept Map

Nature's Balance

Make a concept map with the answers to the Big Question:
What happens when nature loses its balance?

things that happen when nature loses its balance

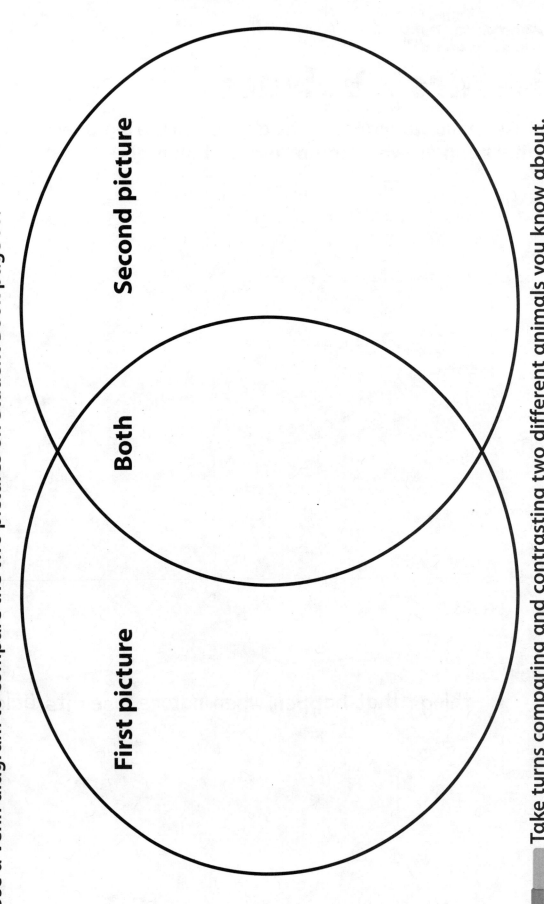

Thinking Map

Comparing Supplies

Use a Venn diagram to compare the two pictures on Student Book page 77.

Second picture

Both

First picture

Take turns comparing and contrasting two different animals you know about.

© Cengage Learning, Inc.

Grammar

The Dog and the Squirrel

Grammar Rules Kinds of Sentences

A **statement** tells something. It ends with a **period**.	Example: *The squirrel eats acorns.*
An **exclamation** shows strong feeling. It ends with an **exclamation mark**.	Example: *Its teeth are so sharp!*
A **command** tells someone to do something. It ends with a **period** or an **exclamation mark**.	Example: *Watch it run up the tree. Hurry up and look!*

Read each sentence. Write the correct, or the best, end mark in the box. Add **S** for a statement, **E** for an exclamation, and **C** for a command.

1. My dog, Barney, chases squirrels ☐ _____

2. He is so crazy ☐ _____

3. Watch him closely ☐ _____

4. I see a squirrel over there ☐ _____

5. Run, Barney, run ☐ _____

6. Don't worry ☐ _____

7. The squirrels always get away ☐ _____

8. Good job, Barney ☐ _____

💬 **Read the sentences to a partner with the correct expression. Pay attention to the punctuation.**

Name _____ Date _____

"It's All in the Balance"

Listen as your teacher reads. Follow with your finger.

1

A village has a beautiful garden filled with colorful flowers, but some of the leaves in the plants have holes. A visitor tells the villagers they must dig up the butterfly bushes if they want to get rid of the holes in the leaves.

2

A boy from outside the village begs the villagers not to dig up the bushes, but they don't listen. They also dig up most of the flowers. The garden is soon a very sad place. The birds, bees, and butterflies are all gone.

3

A villager sees the boy's beautiful garden and asks for his help. The boy tells the man to listen to the bees. The bees tell the man that the villagers upset the balance of nature and that they need to plant new bushes and flowers. The villagers plant them and the garden is soon beautiful once again. When the visitor returns, the villagers chase him away.

Grammar

What's the Question?

Grammar Rules Questions	
For questions with short answers, use **Who**, **What**, **Where**, or **When**.	Example: **What** is your name? *My name is Emily.*
For Yes/No questions, use **Is**, **Are**, **Do**, and **Does**.	Examples: **Are** you in the third grade? Yes, I am. **Do** you speak French? No, I don't.

1. Toss a coin with a partner. Heads moves 1 space. Tails moves 2 spaces.
2. Use the words in the square to ask your partner a question. Your partner answers the question.

When is ____?	Does our school ____?	Do you ____?	What is ____?
Does a dog ____?			Is today ____?
Where is ____?			**Begin**
Are these books ____?	Is your name ____?	Who is ____?	**End**

Now ask and answer three questions about school with a partner.

Unit 2 | Nature's Balance

"It's All in the Balance"

Use a Venn diagram to compare the visitor and the boy from outside the village.

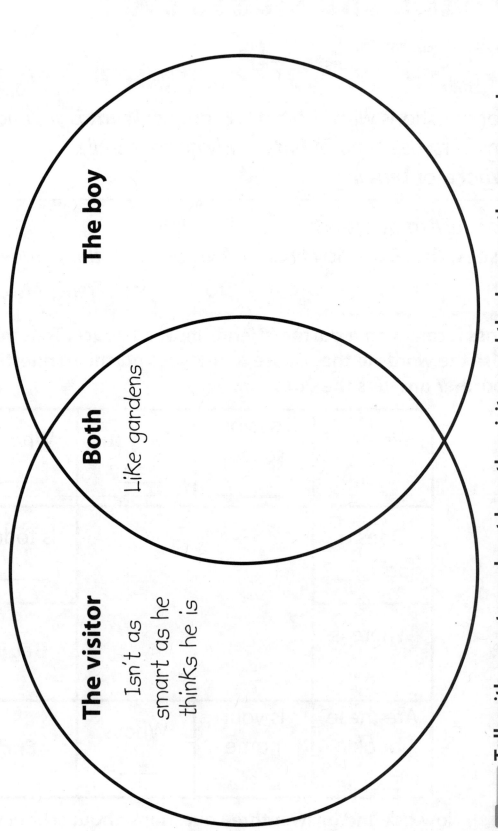

The boy

Both

Like gardens

The visitor

Isn't as smart as he thinks he is

Talk with a partner about how the visitor and the boy are the same and how they are different.

Phonics Practice

Vowel Sounds and Spellings: *u_e*

fl<u>u</u>t<u>e</u>   t<u>u</u>b<u>e</u>

Read each word. Circle the word that names the picture.

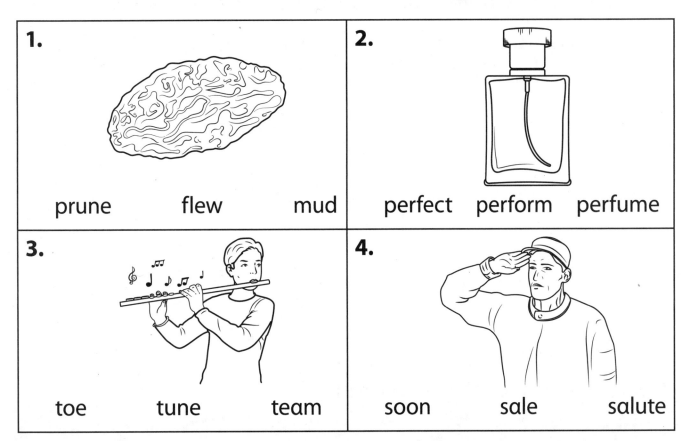

1.

prune   flew   mud

2.

perfect   perform   perfume

3.

toe   tune   team

4.

soon   sale   salute

Read the sentence. Underline the words that have the vowel sound you hear in the word *tube*. Then choose two words and write sentences of your own.

During my concert in June, I will play this tune on my flute.

Fluency

"It's All in the Balance"

Use this passage to practice reading with proper expression.

"What do butterflies know?" the villagers repeated.   7

They dug up all the bushes and laughed at the boy as he   20

sadly walked away.   23

But the boy saved one of the butterfly bushes and took it   35

back to his home. The butterflies and the birds, angry with   46

the villagers, went with him.   51

From "It's All in the Balance," page 91

Expression

B ☐ Does not read with feeling.   A ☐ Reads with appropriate feeling for most content.

I ☐ Reads with some feeling, but does not match content.   AH ☐ Reads with appropriate feeling for all content.

Accuracy and Rate Formula

Use the formula to measure a reader's accuracy and rate while reading aloud.

_____ – _____ = _____
words attempted   number of errors   words correct per minute
in one minute   (wcpm)

Name _____   Date _____

"Animals, More or Less"

Complete a dialogue journal as you read "Animals, More or Less."

What I think	What my partner thinks
Page _____ _____ _____ _____ _____	_____ _____ _____ _____ _____
Page _____ _____ _____ _____ _____	_____ _____ _____ _____ _____
Page _____ _____ _____ _____ _____	_____ _____ _____ _____ _____

Tell a partner which riddle you liked the best. Explain why it was funny.

Name _____ Date _____

Compare Genres

Use a checklist chart to compare a humorous story and a riddle.

	Humorous story	Riddle
funny	✓	✓
usually long		
short		
playful language		
paragraphs		
questions and answers		

🟦 Talk with a partner about which kind of humorous selection you liked better—the story or the riddles. Tell your partner why you liked one more than the other.

"Food for the Birds"

Grammar Rules Kinds of Sentences

A **statement** tells something.	Example: *I have a pet bird*.
An **exclamation** shows strong feeling.	Example: *He is so funny!*
A **command** tells someone to do something.	Example: *Look at this picture of him.*
A **question** asks something.	Example: *Do you have a pet?*
Sometimes the answer to a question has a **contraction**.	Example: *No, I **don't**. No, it **isn't**.*

Read each sentence. Write **C** for command, **S** for statement, **E** for exclamation, and **Q** for question. Then underline the contractions.

1. Do you like corn? _____

2. No, I don't. _____

3. I really love corn! _____

4. Some birds like it, too. _____

5. Where do they find corn? _____

6. Look at the bird feeder. _____

7. Wow! It's full of corn! _____

Write a statement, a question, and an exclamation about something that happened today. Read your sentences to a partner.

Name _____ Date _____

Ecosystem Alert

Make a cause-and-effect diagram of an ecosystem that is out of balance.

Cause	Effect

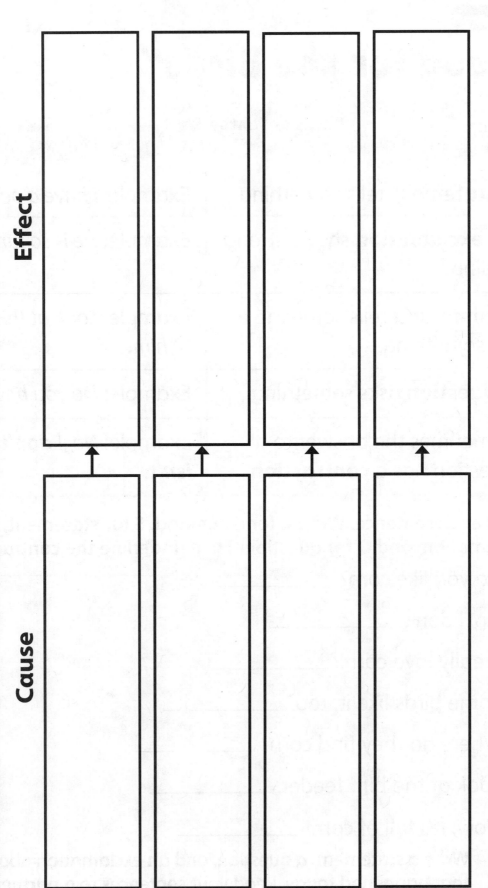

Use your diagram to tell a partner about one cause and its effect shown on Student Book page 111.

Grammar

All About Bears

Grammar Rules Compound Sentences

You can make a compound sentence by joining two short sentences. Use a comma (**,**) + a joining word (**and**, **but**, **or**).

Examples: *Bears eat berries***, and** *they also eat fish.*

*An adult bear is very tall***, but** *a baby bear is much shorter.*

*Bears can walk on four legs***, or** *they can walk on two legs.*

Combine each pair of sentences into one compound sentence. Use the joining word in parentheses.

1. Bears look cute. They are dangerous. (but)

_____

2. You can see bears in a zoo. You might see one in the woods. (or)

_____

3. Bears catch fish in their paws. They eat as many as they can. (and)

_____

4. It is fun to see wild animals. Don't go too close to them. (but)

_____

Tell a partner about two kinds of animals you know about. Use compound sentences.

Name _____ Date _____

"When the Wolves Returned"

Listen as your teacher reads. Follow with your finger.

1

Yellowstone Park is a very special place in northwestern Wyoming. It has many natural wonders.

Many animals live in Yellowstone. There are elk, deer, and wolves. People liked seeing the elk and deer, but the wolves ate many of these animals.

2

The people that ran the park gave money to hunters to kill the wolves. They did not know that this would change many things.

Without the wolves, there were too many elk and coyotes. Because there were too many coyotes, other animals started to disappear. Many animals could not find food or places to live.

3

Scientists said that the problems started when the wolves left Yellowstone. They brought back the wolves.

Now, the other animals are surviving. They have food and places to live. Yellowstone is a balanced ecosystem again.

Grammar

Spin a Sentence

Grammar Rules Compound Sentences: Coordinating Conjunctions

Use **and** to join ideas that are alike.
Use **but** to join ideas that show a difference.
Use **or** to show a choice.

1. Play with a partner.

2. Spin the spinner. Read the sentence.

3. Add another idea that is alike, different, or shows a choice. Use **and**, **but**, or **or** to make a compound sentence.

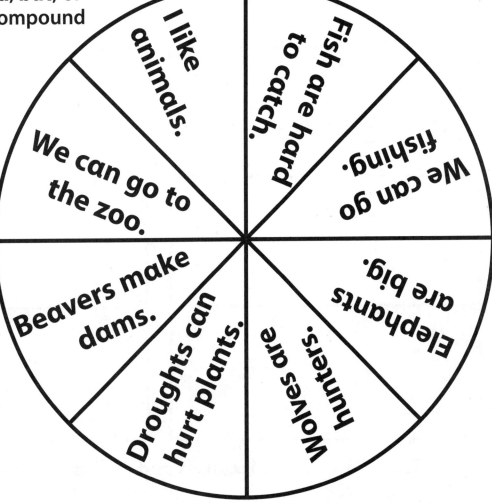

Make a Spinner

1. Place one loop of a paper clip over the center of the circle.

2. Push a sharp pencil through the loop and the paper.

3. Spin the paper clip around the pencil.

"When the Wolves Returned"

Complete this cause-and-effect diagram as you reread "When the Wolves Returned."

Cause		Effect
Park officials got rid of the wolves.	→	The number of elk increased.
Coyotes became the main predators in the park.	→	
	→	
	→	
	→	

Tell a partner about causes and effects in the text that surprised you.

Phonics Practice

Vowel Sounds and Spellings: oo

  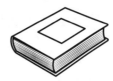

f<u>oo</u>t   b<u>oo</u>k

Read each word. Circle the word that names each picture.

1.	2.
good gone glove	brought broke brook
3.	4.
caddy cookie coat	hook hug hot

Read the sentences. Write the words with the vowel sound you hear in the word *flute* in the first column. Write the words with the vowel sound you hear in the word *foot* in the second column.

1. The cook will use a spoon.
2. Catch a fish with a hook.
3. My birthday is in June.
4. The band will play a tune.

Name _____   Date _____

"When the Wolves Returned"

Use this passage to practice reading with proper phrasing.

The purpose for making Yellowstone a national park was to   10

protect its natural wonders for visitors. People enjoyed seeing   19

animals, like elk and deer, in the park too. But wolves fed on   32

them. So, hunters were paid to kill the wolves. Park officials did   44

not understand that killing the wolves would throw nature out   54

of balance.   56

From "When the Wolves Returned," page 121

Phrasing

B ☐ Rarely pauses while reading the text.   A ☐ Frequently pauses at appropriate points in the text.

I ☐ Occasionally pauses while reading the text.   AH ☐ Consistently pauses at all appropriate points in the text.

Accuracy and Rate Formula

Use the formula to measure a reader's accuracy and rate while reading aloud.

_____ − _____ = _____
words attempted   number of errors   words correct per minute
in one minute   (wcpm)

"Megafish Man"

Complete a reflection journal as you read "Megafish Man."

Page	My question	The answer

Tell a partner which answer or fact was most interesting and why.

Name _____   Date _____

Compare Ecosystems

Use the comparison chart to compare Yellowstone Park and
Mekong River.

Yellowstone Park	Mekong River
Is in the United States	Is in Cambodia

 Tell a partner which ecosystem you would rather visit and why.

Grammar

Pets for Adam

Grammar Rules Compound Sentences

You can use **and**, **but**, or **or** to combine two short sentences into one long compound sentence.

1. Use **and** to join ideas that are alike.
   *Dogs are friendly, **and** they make good pets.*

2. Use **but** to join ideas that are different.
   *Dogs like to be with people, **but** cats often like to be alone.*

3. Use **or** to join ideas that show a choice.
   *You might like to have a dog, **or** you might rather have a cat.*

Use and, but, or or to complete each compound sentence.

Adam loves animals, ____*and*____ he has several pets. His dog sleeps in the kitchen, _____ his two cats sleep there too. Some dogs and cats fight each other, _____ his play together every day. Adam wants to get a snake, _____ maybe he would choose a lizard instead. He asked his mother to buy a snake for him, _____ she said no. She doesn't like snakes, _____ she doesn't want another pet. Maybe Adam should ask again, _____ maybe he should just visit the zoo!

Tell a partner about different kinds of pets. Use compound sentences.

Name _____   Date _____

Ideas

Writing is well-developed when the message is clear and interesting to the reader. It is supported by details that show the writer knows the topic well.

	Is the message clear and interesting?	Do the details show the writer knows the topic?
4 Wow!	❑ All of the writing is clear and focused. ❑ The writing is very interesting.	❑ All the details tell about the topic. The writer knows the topic well.
3 Ahh.	❑ Most of the writing is clear and focused. ❑ Most of the writing is interesting.	❑ Most of the details are about the topic. The writer knows the topic fairly well.
2 Hmm.	❑ Some of the writing is not clear. The writing lacks some focus. ❑ Some of the writing is confusing.	❑ Some details are about the topic. The writer doesn't know the topic well.
1 Huh?	❑ The writing is not clear or focused. ❑ The writing is confusing.	❑ Many details are not about the topic. The writer does not know the topic.

Cause-and-Effect Diagram

Use the cause-and-effect diagram to list the important ideas for your summary.

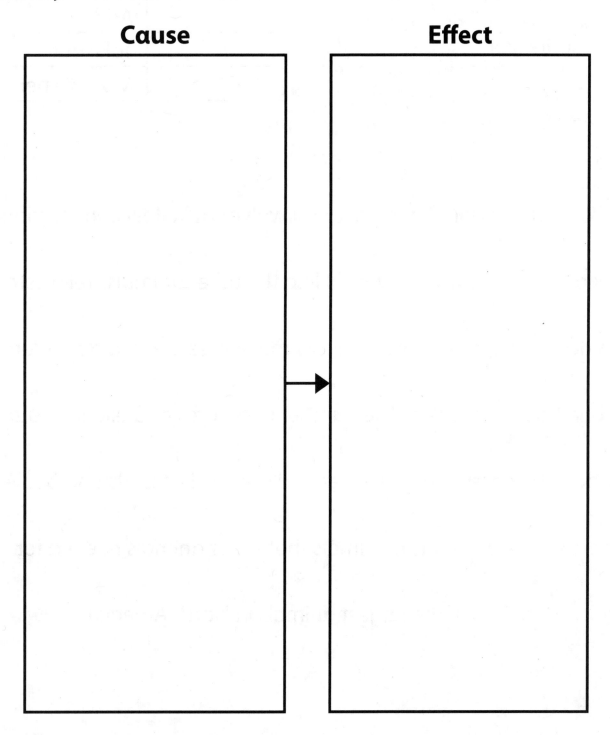

Cause   **Effect**

Name ______________________ Date ______________

Writing Project

Revise

Use revision marks to make changes to this paragraph. Look for:

- **information that doesn't tell about the topic**
- **information that tells about the beginning, middle, and end of the selection**

Revision Marks	
^	Add
ϑ	Take out
⊂⊃→	Move to here

Park officials hired hunters to kill wolves at Yellowstone National Park because the wolves were killing the other animals. Yellowstone is in northwestern Wyoming. Killing the wolves created a problem no one had counted on. The number of coyotes and elk grew out of control. They destroyed the trees and shrubs that birds and beavers need to survive. They ate animals that other animals needed for food. Elk are one of the largest animals in North America.

Edit and Proofread

Use revision marks to edit and
proofread this paragraph. Look for:

- **correct compound sentences**
- **correct contractions**

Revision Marks	
^	Add
⌐	Take out
⌐⌐	Move to here
⌐	Insert comma
⌐	Insert apostrophe

Park officials in Yellowstone did'nt use to think wolves in the

park were useful but now they do. In 1926, the last wolves in the

park were killed. The number of elk increased. Park rangers had

to trap them or they had to hunt them. The number of coyotes

also increased and they ate food other animals needed. Scientists

realized that the park officials had made a mistake, so they brought

wolves back into Yellowstone. The officials willn't let the ecosystem

get unbalanced again.

Name _____ Date _____

Life in the Soil

**Make a concept map with the answers to the Big Question:
What is so amazing about plants?**

Amazing things about plants

Thinking Map

Steps in a Plant's Life

Make a sequence chain to describe the events in a plant's life.

1.

↑

2.

↑

3.

↑

4.

Use your sequence chain to describe a plant's life cycle to a partner.

Grammar

Too Many Rose Blossoms!

Grammar Rules Plural Nouns

1. To make plural forms of most nouns, add **-s**.
   Examples: *sprout* → *sprout**s***   *day* → *day**s***

2. To make plural forms of nouns that end in **x**, **ch**, **sh**, **ss**, **z**, and sometimes **o**, add **-es**.
   Examples: *inch* → *inch**es***   *potato* → *potato**es***

3. To make plural forms of nouns that end in a consonant plus **y**, change the **y** to **i**, and add **-es**.
   Example: *baby* → *bab~~y~~ i + **es** = bab**ies***

Fix each mistake. Write the plural form of each underlined noun.

1. My family likes rose <u>garden</u> a lot! _____

2. We visited two <u>city</u> with rose gardens last week. _____

3. One city garden had 20 different kinds of rose <u>bush</u>! _____

4. Each rose bush had too many <u>blossom</u> to count. _____

5. We met two other <u>family</u> that like rose gardens, too. _____

6. They said they had visited 10 rose gardens in two <u>day</u>. _____

▬▬ **Tell a partner about a plant you have seen. Use two of the plural nouns above.**

"Hoa's Little Garden"

Listen as your teacher reads. Follow with your finger.

1

Hoa is a girl who loves flowers. She dreams of planting her own garden, but the apartment she lives in is very small. Hoa brings home a plant from school, but it dies. Her mom says the plant needed more light.

2

Hoa sees sunlight shining on her balcony. Her mom says there's only enough room for one plant. Hoa plants passion fruit seeds because it will give them fruit *and* flowers. After weeks of checking, Hoa finally sees a little sprout.

3

Hoa's sprout turns into a vine. It spills out of the pot. Soon, the vine grows so much, it grows onto the neighbor's balcony! Hoa, her family, and her neighbor are very happy. They all have sweet, juicy passion fruit to eat.

Hoa plans to grow red chilies next.

Grammar

Day in the Park

Grammar Rules Nouns and Articles

1. Use **a** or **an** to talk about something in general.
   Before a noun that starts with a consonant sound, use **a**.
   Examples: **a** *plant*   **a** *garden*   **a** *person*
   Before a noun that starts with a vowel sound, use **an**.
   Examples: **an** *ant*   **an** *idea*   **an** *ocean*
2. Use **the** to talk about something specific.
   Examples: **the** *boy next door*   **the** *plant by my window*

Add the correct article before each noun.

On Saturday, I had _____ idea for a fun day! _____ friend

and I walked to Hunters Park. We like _____ park a lot. We saw

many beautiful plants in _____ garden there. We saw _____

orchid plant and _____ rose bush. We saw _____ otter in

_____ park, too. It was a great day in _____ park!

🔲🔲🔲 **Tell a partner about a place you like. Use each of the three articles in your sentences.**

Vocabulary Bingo

Play Bingo using the Key Words from this unit.

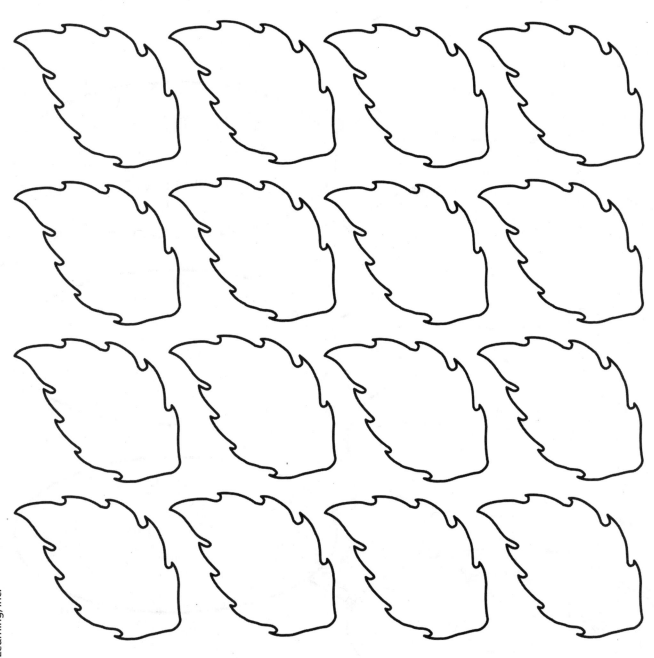

Reread and Retell

"Hoa's Little Garden"

Make a sequence chain to describe the events in "Hoa's Little Garden."

1. Hoa brings home a bean plant from school.

2. The plant dies because there's not enough sunlight in Hoa's apartment.

3.

4.

5.

6.

7.

Use your sequence chain to retell the story to a partner.

Phonics Practice

Review: Two- and Three-Letter Blends

<u>cr</u>ab   <u>gl</u>obe   <u>str</u>eam   de<u>sk</u>

Draw a line between the correct blend and the rest of the word to name each picture. Then write the complete word on the line.

1. str etch scr _____	**2.** sl ate sk _____
3. cr ow gr _____	**4.** fl oves gl _____
5. str ipes spr _____	**6.** sl di sk _____

Read the sentences. Underline the words with blends.

1. The sky is very nice at dusk.

2. Do you stretch before you skate?

Fluency

"Hoa's Little Garden"

Use this passage to practice reading with proper expression.

"Mom!" called Hoa. "Come look. The sun is shining on our 11

balcony. I can have a garden!" 17

Her mom laughed. "Well, maybe you can have a *small* garden," 28

she said, "a *very* small garden. You can grow one plant in a pot. 42

But that's it. There is no space for more than one pot." 54

From "Hoa's Little Garden," page 166

Expression

B ☐ Does not read with feeling.   A ☐ Reads with appropriate feeling for some content.

I ☐ Reads with feeling, but does not match content.   AH ☐ Reads with appropriate feeling for all content.

Accuracy and Rate Formula

Use the formula to measure a reader's accuracy and rate while reading aloud.

$$ \frac{\rule{3cm}{0.4pt}}{\text{words attempted in one minute}} - \frac{\rule{3cm}{0.4pt}}{\text{number of errors}} = \frac{\rule{3cm}{0.4pt}}{\text{words correct per minute (wcpm)}} $$

Name _____ Date _____

"Gifts from the Earth"

Complete the double-entry log as you read "Gifts from the Earth."

What I read	What it means to me
Page _____ _____ _____ _____ _____	_____ _____ _____ _____ _____
Page _____ _____ _____ _____ _____	_____ _____ _____ _____ _____
Page _____ _____ _____ _____ _____	_____ _____ _____ _____ _____

Tell a partner which poem was your favorite and why.

3.10

Compare Genres

Use a Venn diagram to compare a story and a haiku.

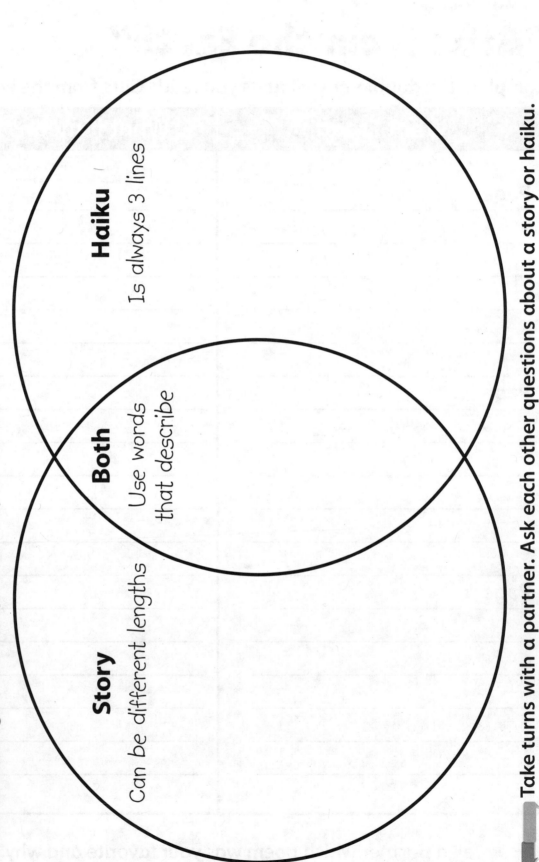

Story

Can be different lengths

Both

Use words that describe

Haiku

Is always 3 lines

Take turns with a partner. Ask each other questions about a story or haiku.

Grammar

Strange Garden Plants

Grammar Rules Plural Nouns

1. For most nouns, make them plural by adding **-s** to the end.
   Example: *sprout* → *sprouts*

2. For nouns that end in **x**, **ch**, **sh**, **ss**, **z**, and sometimes **o**, add **-es**.
   Examples: *branch* → *branches*   *fox* → *foxes*

3. For nouns that end in a consonant plus **y**, change the **y** to **i** and add **-es**. For nouns that end with a vowel plus **y**, just add **-s**.
   Examples: *cherry* → *cherries*   *boy* → *boys*

Write the plural nouns.

My grandmother has a strange garden. She has ___*boxes*___ full of
                                                (box)
_____ all over her deck. She has _____ of _____ growing
(sprout)   (bunch)   (daisy)
in old boots, and _____ in coffee cans. Colored _____ make
                  (lily)   (glass)
pretty vases. They line her windowsills. _____ curl around her
                                         (Vine)
garden swings and _____ . She also made strange metal
                  (bench)
_____ . She stuck them in the ground between the _____ .
(flower)   (bush)
Yes, her garden is odd. I love the _____ I spend there.
                                   (day)

▭ **Pick two plural nouns from the paragraph above and write new sentences. Read them to a partner.**

Thinking Map

Main Idea and Details

Make a main idea and details diagram for rainforest plants.

Main idea:

Detail:
Detail:
Detail:

 Talk about the main idea with a partner. What two details do you think are the most interesting?

Grammar

The Perfect Rainforest Animal

Grammar Rules Count and Noncount Nouns

Count nouns name things that can be counted. These nouns have a singular form and a plural form.

Examples: *papaya* → *papayas* *cloud* → *clouds* *game* → *games*

Noncount nouns name things that cannot be counted. These nouns have only one form.

Examples: *milk   food   water   love   sugar*

Fill in each blank with the correct form of the noun.

1. Okapis are perfect _____ for the rainforest.
   (animal)

2. The _____ that falls every day slides off the okapi's fur.
   (rain)

3. Shadows and _____ create light and dark places.
   (sunlight)

4. An okapi's stripes blend in with the _____.
   (sunlight)

5. Male okapis have short _____.
   (horn)

6. Short _____ do not get caught in the vines and bushes.
   (horn)

7. Okapi mothers produce a lot of _____ for their babies.
   (milk)

8. Adult okapis get all the _____ they need from the rainforest.
   (food)

   Tell a partner something you know about the kind of weather you like. Use two of the nouns above.

"A Protected Place"

Listen as your teacher reads. Follow with your finger.

1

The Okapi Reserve

The Okapi Reserve is a tropical rainforest in the Congo. It has a lot of plants that do not grow anywhere else. The people that started the reserve wanted to protect many different plants and animals.

2

A Home for Animals and Humans

These are some of the animals that live in the reserve. Some of the animals live on the ground. Some of them live in the trees. People live in the reserve, too.

3

A Brave Man

Corneille Ewango is a scientist. He works on the reserve. He loves the forest and its plants and animals. He believes that more scientists and young people should understand the rainforests in the Congo.

Grammar

People of the Reserve

Grammar Rules Common and Proper Nouns

1. A **common noun** names any person, place, thing, or idea. It starts with a lowercase letter.

2. A **proper noun** names a particular person, place, or thing. It starts with a capital letter.

   A short way to write a person's title starts with a capital letter and ends with a period.

	Common noun	Proper noun
person	man/woman	Mr. Ewango
place	country	Congo
thing	forest	Ituri Forest

Circle the common or proper noun that belongs in each blank.

1. People live in _____ in many parts of the world. (rainforests/ Ituri Forest)

2. The _____ are a special group of people. (people/Mbuti Pygmies)

3. They live in the Okapi Reserve in the _____. (country/Congo)

4. The people, plants, and animals of the _____ were once in danger. (forest/Okapi Reserve)

5. _____ and other people are working to save the Okapi Reserve. (A scientist/Mr. Ewango)

Reread and Retell

"A Protected Place"

Make a main idea and details diagram for "A Protected Place."

Main idea:
The Okapi Reserve is an amazing place, full of amazing plants.

Supporting detail:

Supporting detail:

Supporting detail:

Supporting detail:

Supporting detail:

 With a partner, use your main idea and details diagram to summarize the article.

© Cengage Learning, Inc.

Phonics Practice

Plurals: -s, -es, -ies

tree + s = trees   dish + es = dishes   puppy - y + ies = puppies

Name each picture. Write the plural form of each word to match the second picture.

1.

1 bush

2 _____

2.

1 fox

2 _____

3.

1 baby

2 _____

4.

1 mat

2 _____

Read the sentences. Write the plural words in the first column. Write the words with blends in the second column.

1. The puppies play with the kitten.

2. I have two brushes.

3. The buses run on my street.

4. Both boys splashed in the pool.

Plurals	Blends

Name _____   Date _____

"A Protected Place"

Use this passage to practice reading with proper phrasing.

They understand everything about the forest, and they rely on it	11
for food, shelter, and clothing.	16
Pygmies travel from place to place to hunt and fish.	26
They don't just catch game, though.	32
They also collect insects, seeds, fruit, and honey to eat.	42

From "A Protected Place," pages 200–201

Phrasing

B ☐ Consistent pauses match appropriate phrasing.   A ☐ Occasional pauses that match appropriate phrasing.

I ☐ Frequent pauses that match appropriate phrasing.   AH ☐ Rare pauses at appropriate points in text.

Accuracy and Rate Formula

Use the formula to measure a reader's accuracy and rate while reading aloud.

$$\underbrace{}_{\substack{\text{words attempted} \\ \text{in one minute}}} - \underbrace{}_{\text{number of errors}} = \underbrace{}_{\substack{\text{words correct per} \\ \text{minute (wcpm)}}}$$

Name _____   Date _____

"Rosie's Reports"

Complete the fact cards as you read "Rosie's Reports."

That's Amazing!

An amazing fact about _____

is _____

That's Amazing!

An amazing fact about _____

is _____

That's Amazing!

An amazing fact about _____

is _____

That's Amazing!

The most amazing fact of all _____

is _____

Tell a partner which fact you think is the most amazing. Explain why you think so.

Compare Text Features

Use a comparison chart to compare a science article and a blog.

"A Protected Place"	"Rosie's Reports"
Feature: Captions **Example**: An okapi runs through the woods.	**Feature**: Captions **Example**: A worker gets ready to wrap a bundle of leaves.
	Feature: Date line **Example**: Date: November 8

 Take turns with a partner. Ask each other questions about the blog and the article.

Grammar

The Make-it-Plural Game

Grammar Rules More Plural Nouns

Add **-s** or **-es** to make most nouns **plural**:

plant → plant**s**   box → box**es**   baby → bab**ies**

For a few nouns, use special forms to show the **plural**:

leaf → **leaves**   foot → **feet**   man → **men**

woman → **women**   child → **children**

1. **Play with a partner.**

2. **Spin the spinner.**

3. **Change the noun to a plural. Say a sentence using the plural noun.**

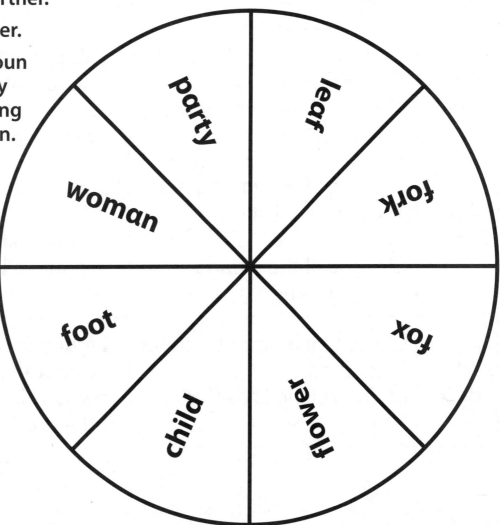

Make a Spinner

1. Place one loop of a paper clip over the center of the circle.

2. Push a sharp pencil through the loop and the paper.

3. Spin the paper clip around the pencil.

Writing Project

Ideas

Writing is well developed when the message is clear and interesting to the reader. It is supported by details that show the writer knows the topic well.

	Is the message clear and interesting?	Do the details show the writer knows the topic?
4 Wow!	❑ All of the writing is clear and focused. ❑ The writing is very interesting.	❑ All the details tell about the topic. The writer knows the topic well.
3 Ahh.	❑ Most of the writing is clear and focused. ❑ Most of the writing is interesting.	❑ Most of the details are about the topic. The writer knows the topic fairly well.
2 Hmm.	❑ Some of the writing is not clear. The writing lacks some focus. ❑ Some of the writing is confusing.	❑ Some details are about the topic. The writer doesn't know the topic well.
1 Huh?	❑ The writing is not clear or focused. ❑ The writing is confusing.	❑ Many details are not about the topic. The writer does not know the topic.

Main Idea and Details Diagram

Complete the main idea and details diagram for your article.

Main idea:

↓

Supporting detail:

↓

Supporting detail:

↓

Supporting detail:

Writing Project

Revise

Use revision marks to make changes
to this paragraph. Look for:
- a topic sentence
- sentence variety

Revision Marks	
∧	Add
℘	Take out
⌒⌐	Move to here
◯SP	Check spelling

Trees are all along the city streets. Grass covers the fields in

the park. Flowers are in pots next to the stores. Weeds even grow

through cracks in the sidewalk

Edit and Proofread

Use revision marks to edit and
proofread this paragraph. Look for:

- **correct spelling of plural nouns**
- **indenting**
- **correct articles**

Revision Marks	
∧	Add
℘	Take out
⬭⤴	Move to here
⬭SP	Check spelling
⏋	Indent

Plants can grow to be many different sizes. Pansys might be just an

few inchs tall. In the desert, a Saguaro cactus can grow to about

40 feet tall. The redwood tree can be over 300 foots tall! It is

amazing how many different sizes plantes can be.

Name _____   Date _____

Let's Work Together

**Make a concept map with the answers to the Big Question:
What's the best way to get things done?**

What's the best way to get things done?

Name _____   Date _____

What's the Message?

Ask a partner to tell you a story. Make a theme chart for the story.

Title: _____

Clues from the Title:

Clues from the Characters:

Theme:

Clues from the Setting:

Clues from the Events:

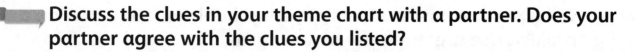 **Discuss the clues in your theme chart with a partner. Does your partner agree with the clues you listed?**

Name _____ Date _____

Food Drive

Grammar Rules Present-Tense Action Verbs

A **present-tense action verb** tells what happens now or what happens often. If the subject of the sentence tells about one other person or thing, add **-s** to the end of most action verbs. For other subjects, do not add **-s**.

Examples: *Tony **buys** eggs.*

*His sisters **buy** milk.*

Fill in the blanks with present-tense action verbs.

Many families need help. Our teacher _____ a food drive
(lead)

to help families. First, Ms. Garcia _____ an advertisement
(write)

about it. Then students _____ canned food from home.
(bring)

Briana _____ the food. Carlos _____ it. Then our teacher
(collect)   (sort)

_____ the food to a local food bank. Many helpers _____
(take)   (work)

together to accomplish something good.

Tell a partner how students at your school work together on a project. Use present tense action verbs.

Name _____   Date _____

"I've Got This"

Listen as your teacher reads. Follow with your finger.

1   Manuel decides to bake a cake for his father's birthday. He has never baked a cake before, so he finds a cookbook with a cake recipe.

    Manuel's sister, Maria, and brother, Luis, offer to help him, but he says, "No thanks. I've got this."

2   Manuel tells his youngest sister, Rosie, that she can't help either. Rosie screams so loudly that Manuel agrees to let her help. Rosie spills the last cup of milk and pours a bag of flour over her head.

    When Luis and Maria return, a sheepish Manuel asks them to help.

3   Luis runs to the market to get more milk. Maria helps Manuel clean the kitchen. The siblings take turns mixing the batter. They put the mixture into the oven. Then the kids wait excitedly for the cake to bake.

    Their dad comes home to a wonderful birthday surprise. Manuel tells their dad that they all worked together.

Grammar

Sentence Match

Grammar Rules Present Tense

The verbs **am**, **is**, and **are** can link the subject of a sentence to a word in the predicate. **Am**, **is**, and **are** are forms of the verb **be**.

Fill in each blank with the correct form of the verb **be**. Then check with a partner to see if your sentences match.

1. I _____ happy at the party.
2. He _____ happy at the party.

3. They _____ ready to play games.
4. She _____ good at playing basketball.

5. You _____ nine years old today.
6. I _____ still eight years old.

7. I _____ his neighbor.
8. We _____ best friends.

 Imagine that you are at a party. Talk with a partner about it. Use sentences with **am**, **is**, and **are**.

"I've Got This"

Make a theme chart for "I've Got This."

Clues from the Title: "I've Got This" makes me think the story is about someone who wants to do things on his own.	Clues from the Characters:
Theme:	
Clues from the Setting:	Clues from the Events:

Compare your theme sentence with a partner's sentence. Then discuss with your partner if both themes apply to the story.

Name _____   Date _____

Syllable Division

dol/phin   ti/ger

Draw a line between the syllables in the words. Circle the word that names the picture.

1. 100	hundred hunter	**2.**	muscle music
3.	added address	**4.**	robot robber
5.	sand sandwich	**6.**	open broken

Read the sentences. Underline each two-syllable word. Then draw a line to divide the syllables.

1. The monkey lives in a jungle.   **3.** The monster was silly.

2. The tiny kitten is cute.   **4.** I have money for a ticket.

Fluency

"I've Got This"

Use this passage to practice reading with proper intonation.

"Hey, big brother," said Maria smiling. "You still *got* this?"   10

"Looks like you could use some help," said Luis.   19

"Well, I'd be done by now if Rosie didn't keep . . .   29

helping," said Manuel.   32

"Oh, so you don't need our help?" asked Maria.   41

"OK, we'll go then."   45

As Luis and Maria turned to leave, Manuel said sheepishly,   55

"Please don't go. Yes, I need your help."   63

From "I've Got This," page 239

Intonation

B ☐ Does not change pitch.   A ☐ Changes pitch to match some of the content.

I ☐ Changes pitch, but does not match content.   AH ☐ Changes pitch to match all of the content.

Accuracy and Rate Formula

Use the formula to measure a reader's accuracy and rate while reading aloud.

_____	−	_____	=	_____
words attempted in one minute		number of errors		words correct per minute (wcpm)

Reading Options

"Ba's Business"

Fill in details from the story in the double-entry log as you read "Ba's Business."

What I read	What it means to me
Page _____	_____
_____	_____
_____	_____
_____	_____
_____	_____
Page _____	_____
_____	_____
_____	_____
_____	_____
_____	_____
Page _____	_____
_____	_____
_____	_____
_____	_____
_____	_____

Tell a partner what you would have done to sell more egg tarts.

Name _____   Date _____

Compare Characters

Use a comparison chart to compare the characters from the two stories.

	Beginning of story	End of story	Why does the character change?
Manuel	He wants to do everything on his own.		
Ba			

◄▬▬▬ **Talk with a partner about which story you liked better and why.**

Grammar

Farmers' Market

Grammar Rules Present-Tense Action Verbs

A **present-tense action verb** must agree with its subject.

Use **-s** at the end of an **action verb** if the subject is **he**, **she**, or **it**.	Examples: *Carmella **loves** street fairs.* *She **takes** me along with her.*
Do not add **-s** to the verb if the subject is **I**, **you**, **we**, or **they**.	Examples: *Buyers **walk** slowly through the fair.* *They **buy** a lot of things.*

Fill in each blank with the present-tense verb form that agrees with the subject.

My parents _____ us to the farmers' market. We _____
      (take)   (enjoy)

all the sights, smells, and sounds. Farmers _____ vegetables
                                                 (sell)

and fruit. One farmer _____ flowers, too. My mother _____
                     (sell)   (buy)

flowers every week. She _____ flowers. One man _____
                         (love)   (cook)

delicious noodles. A woman _____ faces. Two men _____
                       (paint)   (carve)

wooden toys. They _____ out to buyers. The farmers' market is
                   (call)

so much fun! It _____ me smile.
          (make)

Choose three verbs from the paragraph above and write new sentences. Read them to a partner.

© Cengage Learning, Inc.

Thinking Map

What Do You Think?

Talk about a subject with a partner and make an opinion chart of your partner's opinion.

Opinion:

Evidence:

Evidence:

Evidence:

Ask your partner questions about his or her opinion.

Name _____   Date _____

Let's Go to the Play!

Grammar Rules Helping Verbs: *can, could, should*

A **helping verb** tells more about the main verb.

• **Can** shows what someone is able to do: *I **can** run fast.*

• **Could** shows a choice or possible action: *I **could** win a race.*

• **Should** shows an opinion: *I **should** practice more first.*

Choose the correct helping verb to complete each sentence. Use the clue at the end of each sentence to help you.

1. Greta ____*should*____ go to the play. (opinion)
   (could/should)

2. You _____ see the play, too. (opinion)
   (should/can)

3. Roberto _____ go with you. (able to)
   (can/should)

4. I _____ go, but I'd rather see a movie. (possible action)
   (can/could)

5. We _____ go to the play next week, though. (choice)
   (could/can)

 Talk to a partner about things the two of you can do, could do, or should do after school.

© Cengage Learning, Inc.

"A Better Way"

Listen as your teacher reads. Follow with your finger.

1

Every year, the Earth loses many trees. They are cut down to make room for farming. This is called slash-and-burn agriculture. People also want to use the trees for wood. The forests are disappearing!

2

Paola Segura and Cid Simões think there is a better way. They want to save trees and help people. They teach farmers how to use the same small piece of land many times.

Farmers live on the land and make money by growing plants. They do not use slash-and-burn agriculture.

3

To make a difference, many farmers need to grow plants this way. Segura and Simões teach one family what to do. That family teaches five other families. Each family will teach five other families.

Segura and Simões call this the 5 x 5 system. Many trees will be saved. Families will live better lives because of sustainable farming.

Grammar

Helping Verb Tic-Tac-Toe

Grammar Rules Helping Verbs: *may, must, has to, have to*

Use **may** to show permission or possibility: *I **may** be late today.*

Use **must**, **has to**, or **have to** to show what someone needs to do.
Examples: *I **must** go to the doctor after school.*
*I **have to** go to the doctor after school.*
*My mother **has to** take me to the doctor after school.*

To draw an **X** in a box, Player A makes a **may** statement. To draw an **O** in a box, Player B makes a **must** statement. The first player to get three **X**s or **O**s in a row wins. Then play again, with Player A making statements with **has to** and Player B making statements with **have to**.

▶ Tell a partner a way to work together on a classroom task.
Use **may** and **must**.

Vocabulary

Vocabulary Bingo

Play Bingo using the Key Words from this unit.

Reread and Retell

"A Better Way"

Make an opinion chart for pages 270–273 in "A Better Way."

Opinion:

Sustainable agriculture is good for the farmer and good for the land.

Evidence:

It lets farmers grow crops on the same land year after year.

Evidence:

Evidence:

 Use the evidence to explain the opinion to a partner.

Phonics Practice

Vowel Sounds and Spellings: al, aw, au

ch**a**lk

p**aw**

l**au**nch

Read each word. Circle the word that names each picture.

1.	clam claw cloud	**2.**	waste wilt walk
3.	half haul hat	**4.**	ball bell bill
5.	other author either	**6.**	straw stow stop

Read the sentences. Underline the words with the vowel sound you hear in the word *paw*. Then sort the words according to how the sound is spelled.

1. I caught a cold.

2. I saw the sun at dawn.

3. I want to talk while we walk.

4. The rocket will launch.

al	aw	au

Fluency

"A Better Way"

Use this passage to practice reading with proper phrasing.

To make a difference, many farmers need to grow crops this way.   12

Segura and Simões use a special plan to teach more farmers. It is   25

called the *5 x 5 System*. First, they teach one family how to grow   39

crops that don't ruin the land. Then that family teaches five new   51

families what they learned. Each new family teaches five more   61

families. Think of all the land that could be saved in the future!   74

From "A Better Way," page 269

Phrasing

| B | ☐ Rarely pauses while reading the text. | | A | ☐ Frequently pauses at appropriate points in the text. |
| I | ☐ Occasionally pauses while reading the text. | | AH | ☐ Consistently pauses at all appropriate points in the text. |

Accuracy and Rate Formula

Use the formula below to measure a reader's accuracy and rate while reading aloud.

$$\underbrace{\text{_____}}_{\substack{\text{words attempted} \\ \text{in one minute}}} - \underbrace{\text{_____}}_{\text{number of errors}} = \underbrace{\text{_____}}_{\substack{\text{words correct per minute} \\ \text{(wcpm)}}}$$

Name _____   Date _____

"The Ant and the Grasshopper"

Complete the forms as you read "The Ant and the Grasshopper."

 Word Detective

New Word: _____

What I think it means: _____

_____

🔍 Clues: _____

_____

📖 Definition: _____

_____

- -

Word Detective

New Word: _____

What I think it means: _____

_____

🔍 Clues: _____

_____

📖 Definition: _____

_____

Use one of your new words in a sentence about the grasshopper or the ant. Tell a partner.

Compare Purposes

Use a comparison chart to compare the authors' purposes in a persuasive article and a fable.

Title	Topic	Author's Purpose
"A Better Way" by Juan Quintana	sustainable agriculture	
"The Ant and the Grasshopper" by Shirleyann Costigan		

➤ Take turns with a partner. Talk about how the authors' purposes are alike or different.

Grammar

What is in the Garden?

Grammar Rules *be/have*; Subject-Verb Agreement

The verbs **be** and **have** are irregular. The subject and verb must agree. Use these correct forms:

I am	We are	I have	We have
You are	They are	You have	They have
He is / She is / It is		He has / She has / It has	

Write the correct form of be or have to complete each sentence. Choose the correct form for the subject.

Jenna and Jake ___have___ a large garden. Jake's favorite vegetable _____ corn. He _____ several rows of corn in the garden. The corn _____ almost ready to harvest. Both Jenna and Jake _____ excited to roast ears of corn. They also grow tomatoes. Tomatoes _____ their mother's favorite vegetable. Jenna planted sunflowers, too. They _____ delicious seeds and pretty blooms.

I _____ planning to help them pick some corn. I _____ a basket I will take with me.

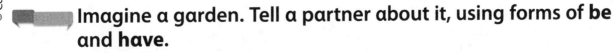 **Imagine a garden. Tell a partner about it, using forms of be and have.**

Ideas

Writing is well developed when the message is clear and interesting to the reader. It is supported by details that show the writer knows the topic well.

	Is the message clear and interesting?	Do the details show the writer knows the topic?
4 **Wow!**	❑ All of the writing is clear and focused. ❑ The writing is very interesting.	❑ All the details tell about the topic. The writer knows the topic well.
3 **Ahh.**	❑ Most of the writing is clear and focused. ❑ Most of the writing is interesting.	❑ Most of the details are about the topic. The writer knows the topic fairly well.
2 **Hmm.**	❑ Some of the writing is not clear. The writing lacks some focus. ❑ Some of the writing is confusing.	❑ Some details are about the topic. The writer doesn't know the topic well.
1 **Huh?**	❑ The writing is not clear or focused. ❑ The writing is confusing.	❑ Many details are not about the topic. The writer does not know the topic.

Opinion Chart

Complete the opinion chart for your persuasive essay.

Opinion:
Evidence:
Evidence:
Evidence:
Evidence:
Evidence:
Evidence:

Writing Project

Revise

Use revision marks to make changes
to these paragraphs. Look for:

- **a clear opinion**
- **supporting ideas**
- **persuasive language**

Revision Marks	
^	Add
ℱ	Take out
⬭⟶	Move to here

We could take meals to people who are housebound. These are

people who cannot, for some reason, leave their homes.

Getting meals would make them feel less lonely. They would also

eat good meals.

We will feel better if we do this.

Writing Project

Edit and Proofread

Use revision marks to edit and
proofread this paragraph. Look for:

- verbs
- subject-verb agreement
- comma after an introductory phrase

Revision Marks	
∧	Add
⌐	Take out
⌐⌐	Move to here
◯ SP	Check spelling
⌒	Add comma

I think that the best thing that our community did was to start

a lunch program for the homeless. At the community center every

Saturday my friends and I serves lunch to twelve guests. Once a

month we also prepare a dinner. It is a good feeling to be able to

help others.

Photographic Credits

1.15 (tl) ZUMA Press, Inc./Alamy Stock Photo. (bl) AP Images/Stefan Rousseau. 2.14 (t) Bruce Raynor/ Shutterstock.com. (c) Brian A Smith/Shutterstock.com. (b) Barrett Hedges/Getty Images. 3.15 (tl) Jabruson/ Nature Picture Library. (cl) Jabruson/naturepl.com. (c) Jabruson/Nature Picture Library. (cr) James H Robinson/Oxford Scientific/Getty Images. (b) The Goldman Environmental Prize. 4.14 (tl) Rhett A. Butler/ Mongabay.com. (cl) REBECCA HALE/National Geographic Image Collection. (cr) bedo/iStock/Getty Images. (b) REBECCA HALE/National Geographic Image Collection.